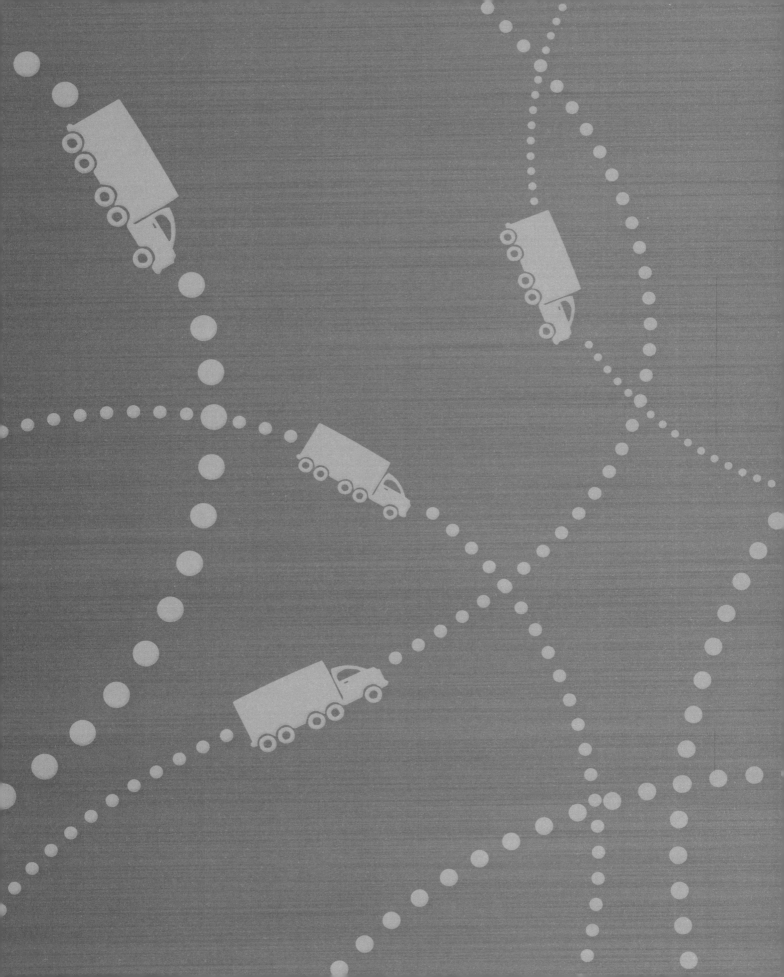

MACHINES AT WORK

Trucks

Clive Gifford

WAYLAND

First published in 2012 by Wayland

Copyright © Wayland 2012

Wayland
338 Euston Road
London NW1 3BH

Wayland Australia
Level 17/207 Kent Street
Sydney, NSW 2000

Editor: Nicola Edwards
Designer: Elaine Wilkinson
Picture Researcher: Clive Gifford

British Library Cataloguing in Publication
Data

Gifford, Clive.
    Trucks. -- (Machines at work)
    1. Trucks--Juvenile literature.
    I. Title II. Series
    629.2'24-dc23

ISBN: 978 0 7502 6889 9

Printed in China
Wayland is a division of Hachette Children's
Books, an Hachette UK company

www.hachette.co.uk

To find out about the author, visit his website:
www.clivegifford.co.uk

Picture acknowledgements:
The author and publisher would like to thank
the following agencies and people for allowing
these pictures to be reproduced:
Cover (main) Michael Stokes / Shutterstock.
com, (inset) Shutterstock © Baloncici;
title page Shutterstock © Chaoss; pp2-
3 Shutterstock © Konstantin Sutyagin;
p4 Shutterstock © Chaoss; p5 (t) tbc, (b)
Shutterstock © Neale Cousland; p6 iStock ©
David Freund; p7(t) tbc, (b) Shutterstock ©
Christine Gonsalves; p8 Shutterstock © Cheryl
Ann Quigley; p9 (t) © Steve Hix/Somos
Images/Corbis, (b) Shutterstock © owen1978;
p10 tbc; p11 (t) tbc, (b) tbc; p12 Shutterstock
© skaljac; p13 Shutterstock © Binkski; p14
Shutterstock © MiloVad; p15 (t) Shutterstock
© Baloncici, (b) Shutterstock © Faraways;
p16 Shutterstock © Maksim Shmeljov; p17 (t)
Michael Stokes / Shutterstock.com, (b); p18
Getty Images; p19 (t) Shutterstock © SVLuma,
(b) Shutterstock © Brendan Howard; p20
Shutterstock © Zoran Karapancev; p21 (t)
Shutterstock © Peter Hansen, (b) Shutterstock
© Dariush M; p23 (t) Shutterstock ©
Faraways, (b) iStock © David Freund; p24
Shutterstock © Maksim Shmeljov

Contents

Trucks on the move

Trucks are large vehicles designed to carry a cargo or load. They are powered by an engine which turns their wheels round. As the wheels turn, they move the truck forward.

Radio antenna so driver can talk to other truckers using a radio

Truck cab, where the driver sits

FAST FACT

The first truck was built in 1896 by a German engineer called Gottlieb Daimler.

Bonnet panel with engine beneath

Headlights light the road ahead when it is dark

ZOOM IN

A flatbed truck (right) stands next to a box trailer truck. The two trucks have the same cab and engine but different areas for carrying different cargoes.

This big truck hauls large loads long distances.

The cab or tractor unit is the front part of a truck. It pulls the trailer, the part that carries the load.

Wheel covered in a rubber tyre

This road train is pulling not one but four heavy trailers. It works in mines in Australia.

Steering a truck

A driver uses a steering wheel to turn a truck. The steering wheel is linked to a truck's front wheels. As the driver turns the steering wheel, the front wheels turn in same direction and the rest of the truck follows.

Mirror shows the view behind the truck

A large ten-wheeler truck turns out of a narrow street. The driver must steer the long vehicle carefully around the corner.

Front wheels turn to the left

ZOOM IN

Before turning the steering wheel the driver checks the road is clear and then flicks a lever at the side of the wheel to make the indicator lights flash.

Drivers can move their trucks backwards. This is called reversing. When a truck is reversing, red lights shine at the back of the truck. The truck may also make a beeping sound to warn drivers and pedestrians.

indicator lights flash to let other drivers know the truck is turning

A worker guides a driver as he reverses his truck to deliver sand to a construction site.

Going uphill

Trucks need a lot of power from their big engines to pull a heavy load behind them. When they travel uphill, they need extra power to climb the slope.

This truck is climbing a steep hill. As the slope gets steeper, more engine power is needed and more fuel is used.

FAST FACT

The massive Caterpillar 797B dump truck uses a lot of fuel. Its tanks hold more than 100 times the amount carried by a hatchback car.

Load stored inside trailer

A truck driver changes to a lower gear to drive uphill. A lower gear makes the engine turn the wheels more slowly but with greater force. Some trucks have as many as 16 gears.

In the cab of this truck the driver has to operate several gear levers.

Rubber tyres grip the road

ZOOM IN

The speedometer dial on the left shows the driver how fast the truck is moving. The fuel gauge on the right shows the driver how much fuel is in the tank.

Driving safely

Trucks are very heavy and move at fast speeds. Such a big, heavy vehicle takes a lot of force to slow it down quickly and safely. This force comes from its brakes.

This truck is being tested to see if it can brake quickly and stop in wet conditions.

ZOOM IN

A brake disc is fixed to the inside of a wheel. The pads press down and rub on the brake disc. This creates a force called friction which slows the wheel down.

Some trucks are fitted with a special gadget that works out the distance between the truck and the nearest vehicle ahead of it. If the truck gets too close, the gadget sounds a warning noise and automatically slows the truck down.

A truck slows down to keep a safe distance from the car in front.

Carrying cargo

Trucks carry an amazing range of loads, called cargo, from cars to chocolate syrup. Garbage trucks remove waste from our homes while tanker trucks carry milk, petrol and other liquids in giant tanks.

Strong metal frame holds cars in place

This truck is called a transporter. It is taking cars from the factory where they were made to showrooms where they will go on sale.

First car to be loaded onto the truck will be the last to be delivered

A container made of steel is lowered onto a truck.

Some trucks carry large boxes called containers. These containers are all the same size. This means they can be filled with many different types of cargo and then carried by ships and trucks all over the world.

FAST FACT

In 2010, the port of Shanghai in China handled 29.05 million cargo containers from ships and trucks – more than any other port in the world.

Loading and unloading

Cargo has to be loaded on to a truck and unloaded at the other end of its journey. Trucks load and unload their cargo in different ways.

Large container behind cab loaded with rock

A digging machine fills a dumper truck with rock. The truck can carry many tonnes of rock from one place to another.

Ladder for driver to climb up into the cab

To unload the cargo, the back of a dumper truck tilts upwards so that it can empty its load behind it. The biggest dump trucks can tip out more than 300 tonnes of earth or rock in just 30 seconds.

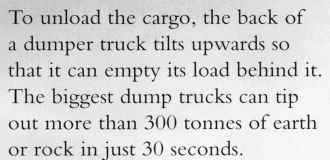

ZOOM IN

A rod called a piston is pushed upwards. It tilts up the back of the dumper truck.

Chunky pattern on tyres helps to grip rough ground

Monster trucks

Some trucks are monsters! These massive machines perform in stunts and obstacle races, launching themselves off ramps and destroying other vehicles in their path.

Driver wears crash helmet

FAST FACT

A monster truck called Bigfoot 5 has the biggest tyres of all. Each tyre is 305cm tall and weighs 1,089kg.

Giant tyres

A brightly-painted monster truck performs in a show.

ZOOM IN

The big gap between the truck's body and wheels allows the wheels to travel upwards when the truck lands after a jump.

A monster truck's giant tyres are not fully filled up with air. This makes them soft and squishy, and allows them to ride over obstacles more smoothly.

A monster truck easily crushes two cars beneath its huge body and wheels.

Strong frame of steel tubes holds wheels and body together

Tow trucks

Some trucks help other vehicles out when they break down, towing them out of danger or back to a garage for repairs. These trucks need powerful engines.

This truck is towing a crashed racing car off the track so it doesn't get in the way during the race.

Flashing amber lights on the cab warn other vehicles

Arm called a boom

Mirrors shows the driver the view behind the towed car

ZOOM IN

The tow truck's wheel lift bar connects to the broken down car. It raises the car's front wheels off the ground as it is towed away.

Tow trucks don't just pull broken down cars. Special trucks called tugs tow airliners carefully around an airport. They help move the airliner safely to the airport buildings.

Fighting fires

Fire trucks rush fire-fighters to a fire or other emergency. They carry equipment to help put out a fire or rescue people in danger.

Giant ladder can stretch upwards to reach the top floors of a tall building

A fire truck races to the scene of a fire. It has a very loud siren and flashing lights to clear the road ahead of traffic so that it can reach the fire more quickly.

TORONTO FIRE

A315

Driver's cab

Toronto Fire

916 5JX   A315

Fire trucks carry fire-fighting tools as well as equipment such as oxygen cylinders to help the people they rescue.

Water is forced up through the hose by powerful pumps in the fire truck so that it can be sprayed on the fire to put it out.

Fire-fighters tackle a blazing fire.

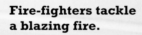

Fire-fighting tools stored in lockers

Large bumper to push through obstacles

FAST FACT

Some fire engines can pump 4,000 litres of water through its hoses every minute.

Quiz

How much have you found out about trucks at work? Try this quick quiz!

1. What type of truck carries liquids such as oil or milk?
a) container truck
b) tow truck
c) tanker truck

2. Who built the first ever truck?
a) Ernest Volvo
b) Gottlieb Daimler
c) Ivor Dumper

3. What is the name of the part of a truck where the driver sits?
a) bonnet
b) trailer
c) cab

4. What happens when a driver reverses a truck?
a) It goes backwards
b) It turns to the left or right
c) It stops

5. What device on a fire engine forces water out of long hoses?
a) the siren
b) the pump
c) the lockers

6. Which monster truck has the biggest wheels of all?
a) Bigfoot 5
b) Maximum Impact
c) Giant Godzilla

7. How long does it take the biggest dump trucks to empty a load of 300 tonnes?
a) 30 seconds
b) three minutes
c) two hours

8. The force of brake pads pressing on a brake disc is
a) thrust
b) gravity
c) friction?

Answers: 1. c, 2. b, 3. c, 4. a, 5. b, 6. a, 7. a, 8. c

Glossary

bonnet a body panel that lifts up to reveal the engine

brake pads pads of material that can press on a brake disc to slow a truck down

bumper a bar made of metal, plastic or rubber which stops a car being damaged if it bumps into something

cab short for cabin, the part of the truck where the driver sits and controls the vehicle

cargo the load carried by a truck

crash helmet a protective hat worn by racing car drivers to stop head injuries if they fall or have a crash

engine the machinery that creates power to turn the car's wheels round

friction the force that slows movement between two objects which rub together

fuel petrol, diesel or another substance that is burned in an engine to create power to make the vehicle go

indicator lights small lights on either side of the truck. One side flashes when the truck is turning in that direction.

obstacles things in a truck's way that it has to drive round or climb over

pedestrians people travelling on foot

road train a large truck which tows two or more trailers over long distances

siren a device which makes a loud sound on fire engines and other emergency vehicles to warn other road users

tow to pull a car or some other object behind a truck

Further Information

Books

Ultimate Machines: Trucks, Rob Colson, Wayland, 2012
Machines Inside Out: Trucks, Chris Oxlade, Wayland, 2012
Motorsports: Monster Trucks, Clive Gifford, Franklin Watts, 2012
Mean Machines: Supertrucks, Paul Harrison, Franklin Watts, 2012
Machines on the Move: Trucks, James Nixon, Franklin Watts, 2010

Websites

http://www.trucksgalore.co.uk/
This website is packed with photos of all sorts of trucks.

http://auto.howstuffworks.com/modern-trucks-channel.htm
A collection of features on different trucks and how they work.

http://www.monstertrucks-uk.com/
A website filled with pictures and information on monster trucks and how they began.

Places

Sheffield Fire & Police Museum. West Bar, Sheffield, South Yorkshire, S3 8PT
http://www.firepolicemuseum.org.uk/
Get up close and explore different fire engines at this city centre museum.

The British Commercial Vehicle Museum. King Steet, Leyland, Lancashire, PR25 2LE
http://www.bcvmt.co.uk/
This museum has a big collection of historic and modern trucks.

Index

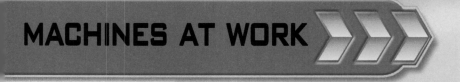

MACHINES AT WORK

Contents of all the titles in the series:

WAYLAND

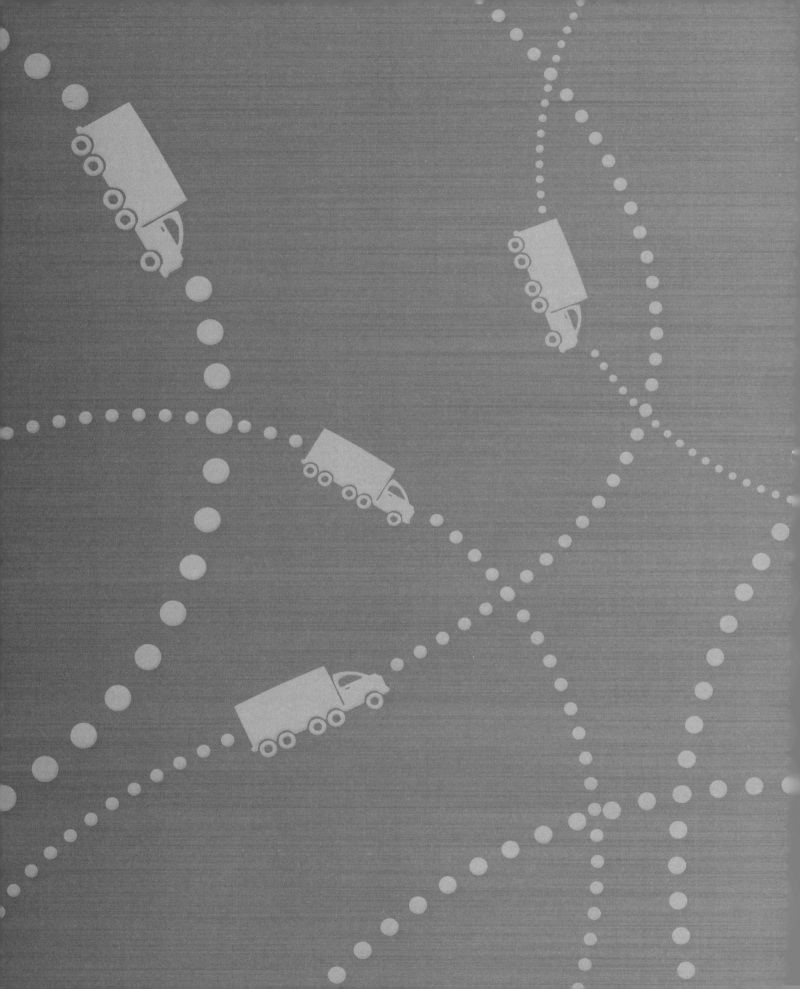